BLAZERS

U.S. MILITARY
ROBOTS

by Barbara Alpert

CONTENT CONSULTANT:
RAYMOND L. PUFFER, PHD
HISTORIAN, RET.
EDWARDS AIR FORCE BASE HISTORY OFFICE

READING CONSULTANT:
BARBARA J. FOX
READING SPECIALIST
PROFESSOR EMERITA
NORTH CAROLINA STATE UNIVERSITY

CAPSTONE PRESS
a capstone imprint

Blazers is published by Capstone Press,
1710 Roe Crest Drive, North Mankato, Minnesota 56003.
www.capstonepub.com

Library of Congress Cataloging-in-Publication Data
Alpert, Barbara.
    U.S. military robots / by Barbara Alpert.
    p. cm. — (Capstone blazers: U.S. military technology)
    Includes index.
    Audience: Grades K to 3.
    ISBN 978-1-4296-8438-5 (library binding)
    ISBN 978-1-62065-211-4 (ebook PDF)
1. Military robots—United States—Juvenile literature. 2. United States—Armed Forces—
Robots—Juvenile literature. I. Title.
UG450.A473 2013
355.8'2—dc23   2012000999

Summary: Describes the robots used by the U.S. military.

Editorial Credits
Brenda Haugen, editor; Kyle Grenz, designer; Laura Manthe, production specialist

Photo Credits
AP Images: Keith Srakocic, 16; DoD photo by Master Sgt. Scott T. Sturkol, USAF, 20-21;
Newscom: MCT/Chuck Kennedy, 14-15, Splash News, 29; U.S. Air Force photo, 12-13, by Mr.
Jim Shryne III, cover (top), Airman 1st Class Jeffrey Hall, 26-27, Noel Getlin, 10, Senior Airman
Julianne Showalter, 22-23, Senior Airman Sarah Stegman, 25, SSGT Dennis J. Henry Jr., 11, Staff
Sgt. Renae Saylock, 5; U.S. Army photo by Spc. Preston Cheeks, cover (bottom), Spc. Joshua E.
Powell, 18, Spc. Theodore Schimdt, 6; U.S. Navy Photo by Kelly Schindler, 19, PH3 Laura A.
Moore, 8-9

Artistic Effects
deviantart.com/Salwiak, backgrounds

Printed in the United States of America in
Stevens Point, Wisconsin.
032012   006678WZF12

TABLE OF CONTENTS

STAYING SAFE

Some jobs are too dangerous for soldiers. Soldiers use robots for these jobs. From a safe distance, soldiers send **remote-controlled** robots to fight or spy on the enemy.

remote-control—a way to control machines from a distance

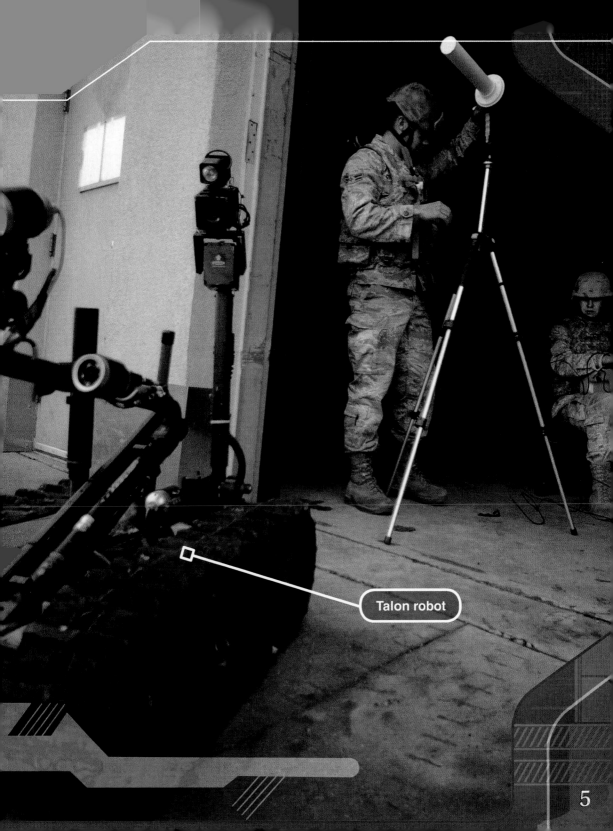

Talon robot

Most of these robots are run by computers. Some robots are operated with a **joystick**, just like a video game.

 The U.S. military uses more than 4,000 robots.

joystick—a control stick

CHAPTER 1

A JOB FOR EVERY ROBOT

WARNING

treads

Ground robots have **treads** like tanks. These robots can climb stairs. Some of these robots have arms to **defuse** bombs.

bomb

tread—a series of bumps and deep grooves on a track

defuse—to take a bomb apart before it explodes

9

Cameras on the All-Purpose Remote Transport System (ARTS) show soldiers what the robot is doing. ARTS can do many things, such as fight fires using a water cannon and act like a bulldozer.

grip controller

camera

ARTS

ARTS can be used like a forklift. It can clear away land **mines**, making the roads safer for soldiers.

mine—an explosive device; land mines are buried underground; water mines float in the water

A Packbot Scout is so small it fits in a backpack. Soldiers roll this robot under vehicles to check for bombs.

 **FACT** iRobot makes the Packbot. The company also sells Roomba robot vacuum cleaners.

Soldiers throw the Dragon Runner robot over walls and through windows. The robot's main mission is to spy on enemies.

 Whether it lands right side up or upside down, the Dragon Runner can spy on enemies.

CHAPTER 2

SPIES IN THE SKY

Unmanned aerial vehicles (UAVs) are flying robots. They fly without pilots into battle zones to keep an eye on enemies.

FACT A soldier tosses the Raven UAV like a football to launch it into the air.

The Global Hawk uses **radar** to spy through the clouds. It is guided by a **global positioning system** (GPS).

Global Hawk

radar—a device that uses radio waves to track the location of objects

global positioning system—an electronic tool used to find the location of an object

MAV

The Air Force is testing micro aerial vehicles (MAVs). MAVs look like birds or insects. These small robot spies will sneak into places unnoticed by the enemy.

CHAPTER 3

FIGHTING MACHINES

The Talon robot can climb stairs and roll over rocky ground. It can shoot rockets and defuse bombs even when it's underwater.

The Reaper Hunter-Killer UAV carries two **missiles**. **Lasers** make sure the missiles hit their targets.

missile

missile—an explosive weapon that can travel long distances

laser—a narrow, powerful ray of light used to guide missiles

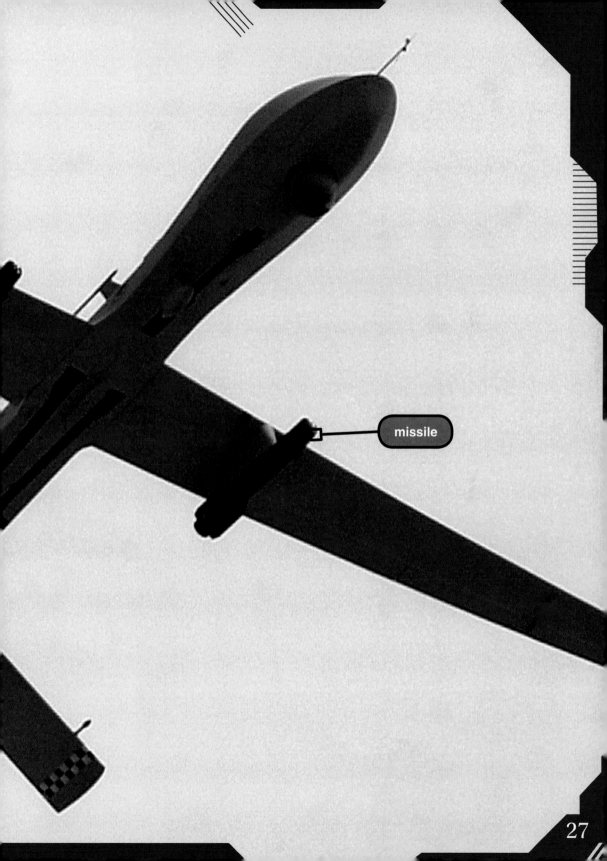

missile

CHAPTER 4

ROBOTS OF THE FUTURE

Soon robots will rescue hurt soldiers on the battlefield. Robots will even be able to fire soldiers' weapons in battle. That will keep soldiers farther from danger.

FACT Robots can work in extreme heat and cold. They can even go into space.

GLOSSARY

defuse (dee-FYOOZ)—to take a bomb apart before it explodes

global positioning system (GLOH-buhl puh-ZI-shuh-ning SISS-tuhm)—an electronic tool used to find the location of an object

joystick (JOI-stik)—a control stick

laser (LAY-zur)—a narrow, powerful ray of light used to guide missiles

mine (MINE)—an explosive device; land mines are buried underground; water mines float in the water

missile (MISS-uhl)—an explosive weapon that can travel long distances

radar (RAY-dar)—a device that uses radio waves to track the location of objects

remote control (ri-MOHT kuhn-TROHL)—a way to control machines from a distance

tread (TRED)—a series of bumps and deep grooves on a track

READ MORE

Dougherty, Martin. *Air Warfare.* Modern Warfare. Pleasantville, N.Y.: GS Learning Library, 2010.

Gifford, Clive. *Robots.* New York: Atheneum, 2008.

Simons, Lisa M. Bolt. *The Kids' Guide to Military Vehicles.* Mankato, Minn.: Capstone Press, 2010.

INTERNET SITES

FactHound offers a safe, fun way to find Internet sites related to this book. All of the sites on FactHound have been researched by our staff.

Here's all you do:

Visit *www.facthound.com*

Type in this code: 9781429684385

Super-cool stuff!   Check out projects, games and lots more at
www.capstonekids.com

INDEX